FACTS ABOUT ME

My name is:_____

I was born in: _____

I now live in: _____

My birthday is: _____

The name of my school is: _____

I am in grade: _____

My teacher is: _____

Things I know about Texas: _____

_____
_____
_____
_____
_____
_____
_____
_____
_____
_____
_____
_____
_____

Places in Texas I would like to visit:_____

_____
_____
_____
_____
_____

Places in Texas I've been: _____

_____
_____
_____
_____

Things I want to learn about Texas:_____

_____
_____
_____
_____

MY TEXAS

There's a saying, "Everything's bigger in Texas!" The land, and how it is formed, is no exception. There are many different aspects to the state's various landforms. These include the following:

mountains	beaches
plateaus	rivers
lakes	valleys
hills	plains
escarpments	basins

Which of these do you see in the area where you live? Circle all of the terms that apply. If you live in a state other than Texas, list landforms in your state that are different from the ones on this list.

_____

_____

_____

The name Texas comes from the Caddo tribe's word meaning "friends" or "allies." Spanish explorers wrote the word as tejas to refer to the Native Americans who lived in East Texas.

Many other places in Texas have names that come from Spanish words. The cities of Amarillo and El Paso are just two examples. Find five landforms or cities with Spanish names and place them on the map. For help, you might consult an atlas, your parents, your teacher, the Internet, or other sources.

The nickname for Texas is "The Lone Star State." This name is a reference to the state flag that has the single star on it. As you have already learned, the one star is very important as it stands for unity as early Texans battled to become an independent land.

Make the border on pages 2 and 3 a patriotic red, white, and blue border.

If you live in Texas, put a star on the map to show where you live.

Mark the map with different shapes to indicate:

1. Where you have lived (or would like to live if you currently live in another state) ●
2. Where you have visited ◆
3. Where you would like to visit ■

Describe your community's location in the state as clearly as you can. Do you live in the Mountains and Basins region? On the Gulf Coastal Plains? Near a river? On the Central Plains?

Explain.

_____

_____

_____

_____

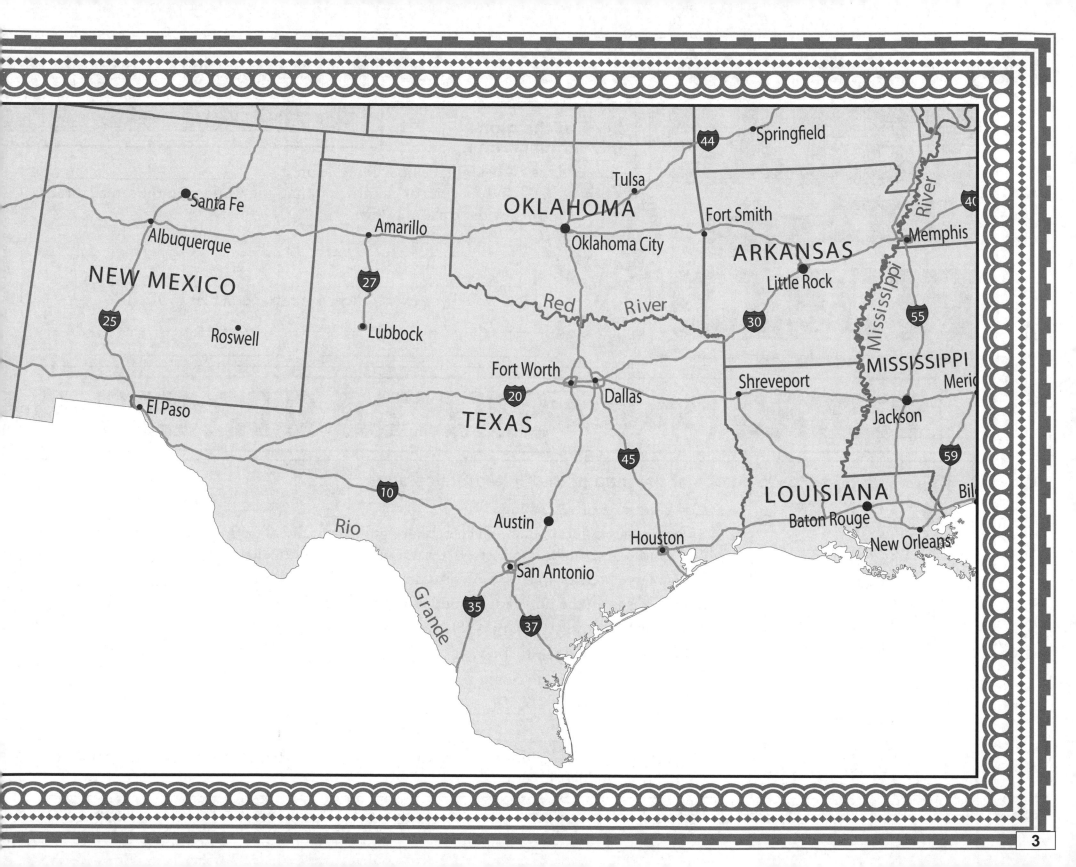

TEXAS AND THE WORLD

Look at the globe in your classroom.

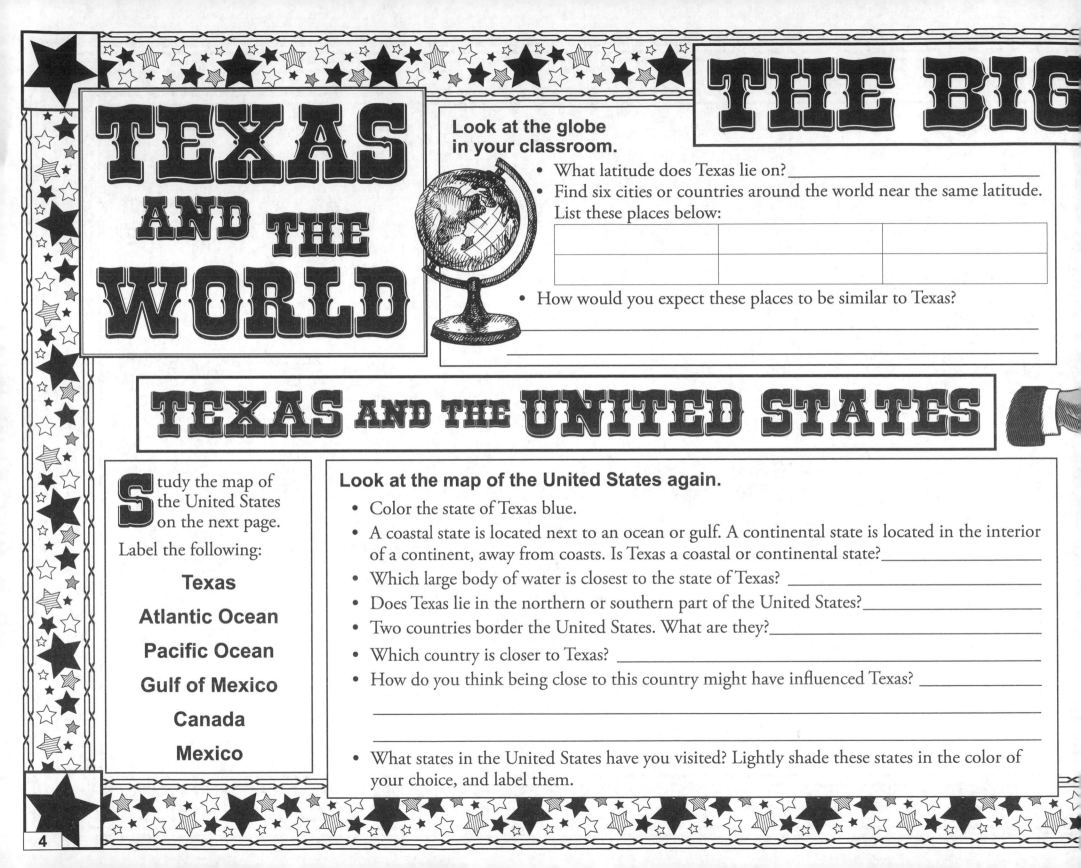

- What latitude does Texas lie on? _____
- Find six cities or countries around the world near the same latitude. List these places below:

- How would you expect these places to be similar to Texas? _____
_____

TEXAS AND THE UNITED STATES

Study the map of the United States on the next page.

Label the following:

Texas

Atlantic Ocean

Pacific Ocean

Gulf of Mexico

Canada

Mexico

Look at the map of the United States again.

- Color the state of Texas blue.
- A coastal state is located next to an ocean or gulf. A continental state is located in the interior of a continent, away from coasts. Is Texas a coastal or continental state?_____
- Which large body of water is closest to the state of Texas? _____
- Does Texas lie in the northern or southern part of the United States?_____
- Two countries border the United States. What are they?_____
- Which country is closer to Texas? _____
- How do you think being close to this country might have influenced Texas? _____
_____
_____
- What states in the United States have you visited? Lightly shade these states in the color of your choice, and label them.

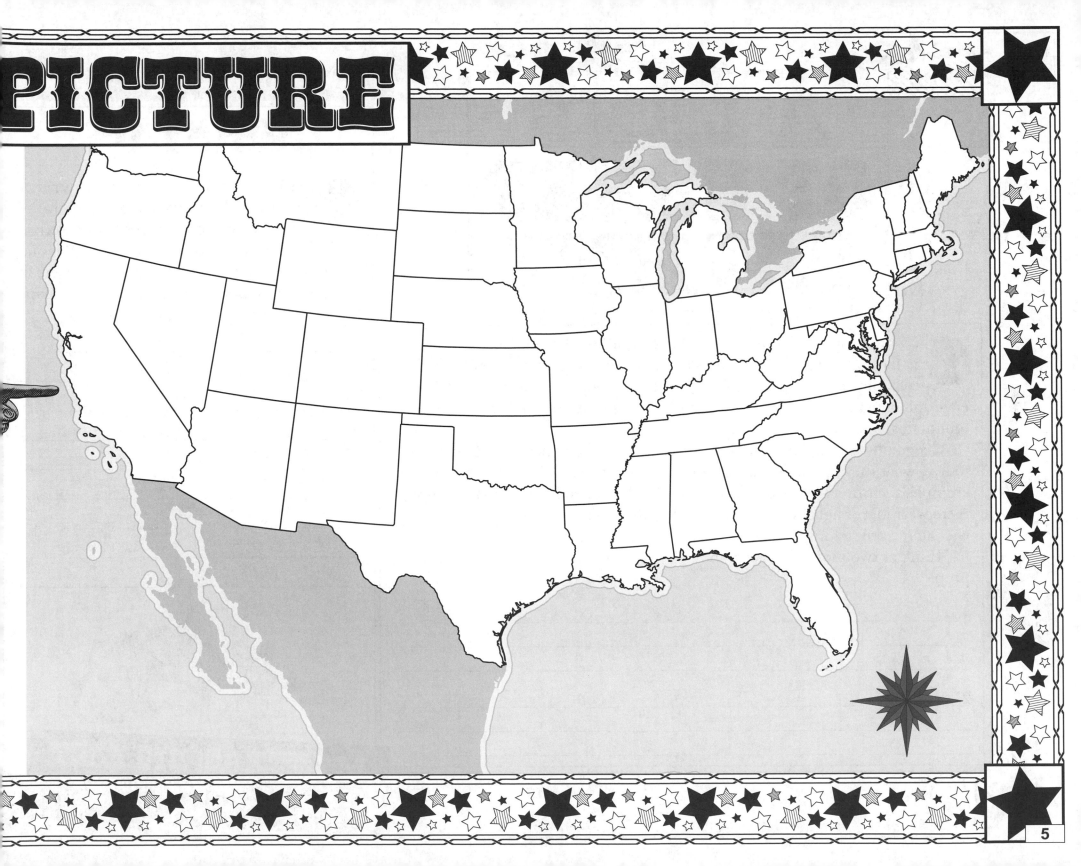

PICTURE

A LAND OF GREAT VARIETY

The word geography comes from a Greek word that means "the study of the Earth." It includes two kinds of study: human geography and physical geography. Human geography looks at how people create and use the environment, and physical geography looks at the landforms of the Earth like mountains, hills, plains, and canyons.

Geography is really important in everyday life. It helps people decide where to live, what they can do for recreation, and what type of jobs they can have. For example, the tropical climate of southern Florida means the residents who live there wear lots of lightweight clothing. They may choose swimming and surfing over alpine skiing for sports.

Think of two more ways geography plays an important role in the lives of people.

1. _____
_____
_____

2. _____
_____
_____

WHAT IF?

Texas is known to have very erratic weather patterns. The summer temperatures in Dallas stay higher than 100° F for weeks. In the winter, the temperature can be 70° F one day and freezing the next! What if Texas were in a tundra? How would life be different for people living in the state? List at least three ways.

1. _____
_____
_____

2. _____
_____
_____

3. _____
_____

MY TEXAS! BIG FACT

The largest city in Texas is Houston. It is the fourth largest city in the United States!

The land of Texas has always shaped the lives of the humans who have lived there. To understand the history of Texas and its people, we must first look at the land.

Texas has four main geographic regions:

Coastal Plains

Central Plains

Great Plains

Mountains and Basins

On the next few pages, you will be exploring all four geographic areas and how they affect the lives of people who live and have lived in Texas.

How does geography affect your life? Give three examples.

1. _____

_____

_____

_____

2. _____

_____

_____

_____

3. _____

_____

_____

Geography Inspires Music

More than 70 years ago, in 1941, June Hershey penned the words to what has become the unofficial song of Texas. The song is played at many Texas sporting events, such as during every seventh inning stretch at the Texas Rangers ballgames.

The stars at night are big and bright
Deep in the heart of Texas
The prairie sky is wide and high
Deep in the heart of Texas

The sage in bloom is like perfume
Deep in the heart of Texas
Reminds me of the one that I love
Deep in the heart of Texas

The coyotes wail along the trail
Deep in the heart of Texas
The rabbits rush around the brush
Deep in the heart of Texas

The cowboys cry, "Ki-yippee-yi!"
Deep in the heart of Texas
The doggies bawl and bawl and bawl
Deep in the heart of Texas

The lyrics of this popular tune express the various attributes of Texas. For example, because much of the land is prairie, stargazing is made easy in the country. The sage plant gives off an aromatic smell. Coyotes howl at the moon. Jackrabbits "rush" at speeds up to 40 miles per hour, and cowboys are synonymous with Texas culture. Now, it's your turn. What do you think a "doggie" is? Hint: Cowboys shared trails with this animal. _____

THE COASTAL PLAINS

There are five distinct areas of the Coastal Plains region. These include the Piney Woods, Gulf Coast Plain, South Texas Plain, Post Oak Belt, and the Blackland Prairie.

The Piney Woods gets its name because it's part of a large forest that stretches all the way from the Atlantic Ocean to Texas. As you can imagine, many people who live in this part of the state work in the lumber industry. The Gulf Coast Plain is where many of Texas's rivers dump out into the Gulf of Mexico. Fishing is an important industry on the Gulf Coast. The South Texas Plain is dry and flat. Farming and ranching are key industries there. The Post Oak Belt is made up of rolling hills and farming is a key industry. The Blackland Prairie is known for its rich soil, again great for farming. Limestone and gravel are important building resources that are found in this area.

Texas is divided into four geographical regions. The largest of these areas, the Coastal Plains, covers roughly one-third of the state. In the far northern part of this region, you could build a snowman, while down south you could build a sandcastle on the beach. From the Gulf of Mexico, the Coastal region reaches inland some 250 miles.

Padre Island, a barrier island that runs along the south Texas coast for 110 miles, is the largest sand beach in the country! It's called a "barrier" because it helps block the mainland from dangerous hurricanes and tropical storms.

Major Cities of the Coastal Plains

Four of the state's largest cities are located in the Coastal Plains. These cities have certain qualities that affect settlement patterns. For example, Houston is referred to as a port city. Ports are places where big cargo ships dock to load and unload supplies. The Port of Houston is a major trade center where foreign countries ship goods to sell in America. San Antonio grew up along the San Antonio River, and today is home to the famous Riverwalk. Dallas, once a frontier trading post, was soon linked to other cities by railroad and is now a major business center. Austin, the capital city of Texas, is also located in this region, and connects with the Colorado River.

What do you think would happen to the populations of these important cities if they weren't located near ports, rivers, or railroads?

_____
_____
_____
_____

Combine the description above with your creativity to draw an icon that could represent the Coastal Plains region.

THE CENTRAL PLAINS

The Grand Prairie is a wide-open grassy land filled with mesquite trees and tall grasses. Texas is known for its cooking, and mesquite smoking is a common way of preparing barbeque, steaks, and many other types of dishes. Located in this region of Texas, Fort Hood is the largest Army base in the United States. The Cross Timbers area of the Central Plains gets its name from all of the oak, hickory, and pecan trees that grow there. Cross Timbers stretches 150 miles from the Red River south to the Colorado River. Finally, the Rolling Plains, the last section of the Central Plains is home to many ranches where you can find cattle, sheep, and goats. Texas has led the U.S. in cotton production for the past 100 years!

Major Cities of the Central Plains

Fort Worth is known for its place in history as a meatpacking center. The "stockyards" are a very popular place to visit for both tourists and locals. Also in this area is the Dallas-Fort Worth international airport, second largest in the country. It has flights to 205 locations around the world.

Why do you think the DFW airport has its own post office, zip code, and postal city designation (DFW Airport, TX)?

_____

_____

_____

Combine the description above with your creativity to draw an icon that could represent the Central Plains region.

MY TEXAS! BIG FACT
King Ranch in South Texas covers 825,000 acres. That's larger than the state of Rhode Island!

One of the unique features of the Central Plains region is its range of elevations, from 750 feet above sea level on its eastern edge to 2,000 feet in the west. Like the Coastal Plains, it too is divided into smaller areas. These include the Grand Prairie, the Cross Timbers, and the Rolling Plains.

A natural region is a large area of land whose places have something in common like landforms or natural resources. Oil and natural gas are common throughout this part of Texas. Common weather patterns occur within regions. The hottest summer temperatures are typically found in the Central Plains.

THE GREAT PLAINS

This section of Texas is roughly 81,500 square miles in size and is known as the Panhandle because of its unique shape. This region is filled with a wide assortment of wildlife including roadrunners, great horned owls, diamondback rattlesnakes, and prairie dogs.

The world's largest concentration of playa lakes is found in this part of Texas. There are nearly 22,000 of these dry lakes in the Great Plains region. The High Plains of this region contains the largest level plain in the United States. Also, special to this region is the Angora goat. This animal's coat is called "mohair" and is spun into fine yarn for clothing and other products. Almost half of the world's mohair comes from this part of Texas.

The Great Plains region of Texas is made up of high, flat grasslands. This is part of the larger Great Plains area of North America that runs from Canada all the way down to Mexico. The Caprock Escarpment is a series of cliffs and slopes that divide the Great Plains from the Central Plains.

This is the coldest region in Texas and home to the Noble Great Plains Windpark, which showcases 76 wind turbines that help convert wind into energy. This pollution-free form of energy creation provides electricity needs for up to 38,000 homes!

MY TEXAS! BIG FACT

More wool comes from Texas than any other state in the U.S. That's a lot of sheep!

There are two major cities located in this region, Amarillo and Lubbock. Amarillo is the Spanish word for the color yellow. Visitors to this area are sure to see the majestic Palo Duro Canyon. This canyon is only second largest behind the famous Grand Canyon and is roughly 60 miles long, 6 miles wide, and, in some sections, nearly 1,000 feet deep. There is also a massive art display near Amarillo called Cadillac Ranch where you will find 10 Cadillacs half-buried in a line. This was to show the evolution of the car's popular tailfins.

Lubbock is home to Texas Tech University and is also part of the largest contiguous cotton-producing region in the world.

MOUNTAINS AND BASINS

Rattlesnakes, peregrine falcons, and mountain lions are just a handful of creatures you might see in this part of the state. The Pecos River and the Rio Grande are two important waterways in the Mountains and Basins region. The McDonald Observatory in the Davis Mountains is a leading center of astronomical research. In this part of the country, deep dark skies abound, making space study easy. One of the world's largest optical telescopes can be found here.

Unique to this region is an unexplained phenomenon known as the Marfa Lights. Named after the West Texas city of Marfa, these mysterious glowing basketball-shaped orbs have been reported to float, dart around, split in two, merge, and flicker in the night sky.

MY TEXAS! BIG FACT

This region is the driest and windiest part of the state. Only 8 inches of rain falls here each year!

This region of Texas is about the size of South Carolina! The Rocky Mountains take up much of this area. As you might imagine, the highest point in Texas is found here. The Guadalupe Peak rises 8,749 feet above sea level. Basins are bowl-shaped landforms that sit between the mountains. What you may not know is that there is even a desert in this part of Texas. The Chihuahuan Desert also stretches into Mexico and covers a total of 140,000 square miles, making it the second largest desert in North America.

Even though there are many towns throughout the Mountains and Basins region, El Paso is the only major city here. It is the fifth-largest city in Texas and is home to Fort Bliss, the largest military training facility in the country. El Paso is the only major Texas city in the Mountain time zone. Franklin Mountains State Park covers 24,000 acres and is the largest urban park in the United States.

El Paso is nicknamed "The Sun City" because the sun shines on average 302 days each year. However, this part of the state also experiences severe thunderstorms that can cause heavy flooding. Also, windstorms have been known to kick up large amounts of sand and dust.

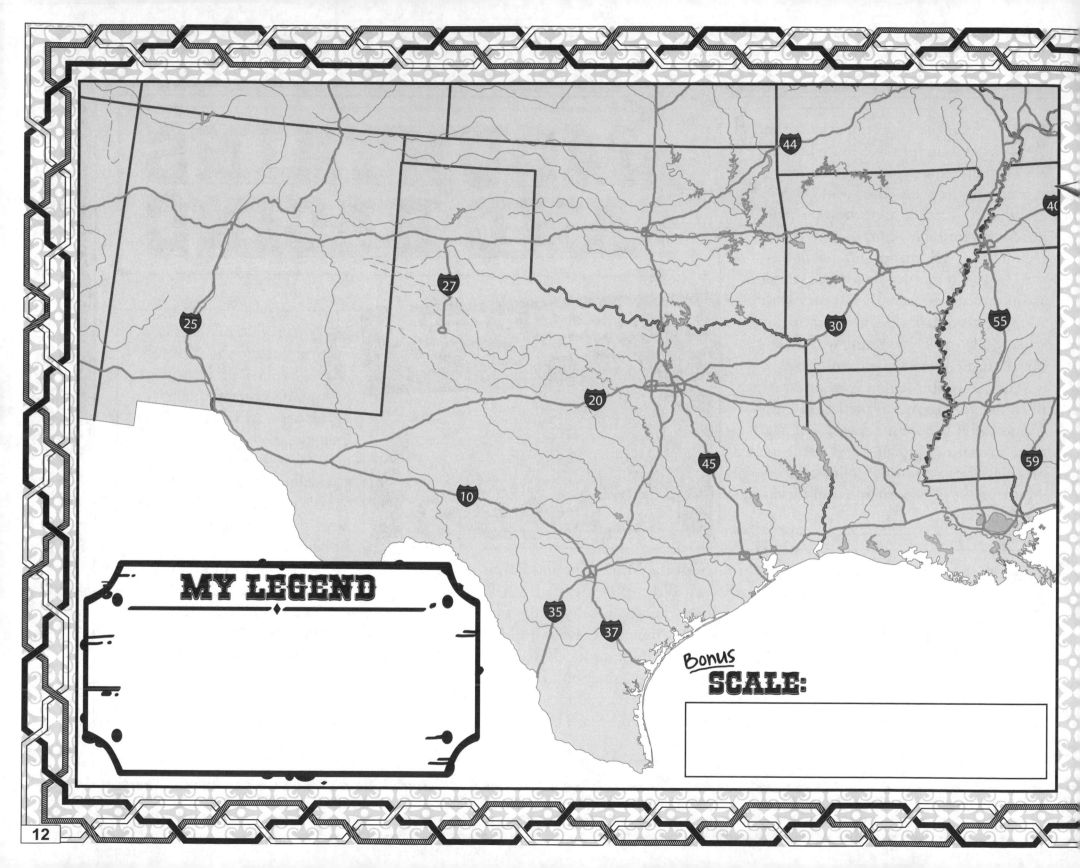

MY LEGEND

Bonus

SCALE:

TEXAS REGIONS

Putting It All Together

1. Use a pencil to mark off the four regions of Texas.

2. Draw and label these major Texas rivers: Red, Trinity, Rio Grande, Sabine, Colorado, Pecos, Brazos, Nueces, San Antonio, Guadalupe, and Neches.

3. Locate (put a dot on the map) and label these major cities: Houston, El Paso, Amarillo, Dallas, Lubbock, San Antonio, Fort Worth.

4. Locate (put a star on the map) and label Austin as the capital of Texas

5. Locate and label the Gulf of Mexico. Color it blue.

6. Label the four states that border Texas.

7. Finally, fill in your legend with the four region names and choose four colors (one for each region).

8. Color each region to match your legend.

MY TEXAS! BIG FACT

Texas is so big that the city of El Paso is closer to Needles, CA, than it is to Dallas! (It takes about 9 hours to drive from Dallas to El Paso.)

Bonus: Create a scale for your region map. A scale tells you how far it is in real miles from one point on a map to another. Here's a hint to get you started: It is about 200 miles from San Antonio to Houston. Take a ruler and measure the distance between these two cities on your map. Let's say it was an inch between cities. Take the ruler and near the bottom of your map, make a line that measures an inch. On the left end, mark a "0" and on the right end mark "200 miles." At the half-inch point, draw a dash and mark it "100."

Using your newly created scale, answer the following:

1. How many miles are there between Houston and Austin?

_____

2. Between Houston and Dallas?

_____

3. Between Dallas and El Paso?

_____

4. Between Fort Worth and Austin?

_____

5. Between Austin and Lubbock?

_____

6. Between Amarillo and El Paso?

CLIMATE AND PRECIPITATION

Climate describes weather patterns over a particular area. Areas that are closer to the Earth's equator are hotter than those places closer to the North and South Poles. Some states are known for beautiful tropical temperatures, while others are popular winter destinations for skiing and snowboarding. Texas, on the other hand, is like a weather buffet. From severe drought to flash flooding, Texas has it all. Tornadoes, hailstones, hurricanes, snow, sleet, and thunderstorms are all part of the weather mix.

Problems With Texas Weather

We've seen how hurricanes and tornadoes can cause major damage to buildings and homes. Weather in Texas can change rapidly, so it is always a smart idea to be prepared. Think about ways you can plan ahead for safety and provision should bad weather come to your part of the state.

Hurricanes

Raging storms with heavy winds and rain are called hurricanes. In 1900, a violent hurricane churned in the Gulf of Mexico and slammed into the Texas coast, making landfall in Galveston. The terrible storm destroyed the city and killed more than 6,000 people. Even though this tragedy happened more than 100 years ago, it is still one of the worst natural disasters in U.S. history.

Tornadoes

Fierce winds that begin to swirl into funnels are called tornadoes. These destructive weather events are filled with rain, debris, and hail. Winds can rip houses off their foundations and toss 18-wheelers around like they are toys. Parts of West-Central Texas are known as Tornado Alley because of the numerous amounts of tornadoes that happen there. Texas ranks first in tornado occurrences with an average of 135 a year.

Northers

Because Texas borders the Gulf of Mexico and the Rocky Mountains lie to the west, the majority of the state is plains that allow air masses to move freely. Warm, water-filled gulf air collides with the Arctic's cool, dry air. Within days, cold air from Canada can race across the country down into Texas. The warm air rushes north, pulling the cold air behind in its wake. It can be 80 degrees in the afternoon, and because of a norther, drop 30 degrees in the span of only a few hours.

MY TEXAS! BIG FACT Caprock Canyons covers more than 13,000 acres of land. It is made up of very rocky ground and is home to the exotic North African Barbary sheep!

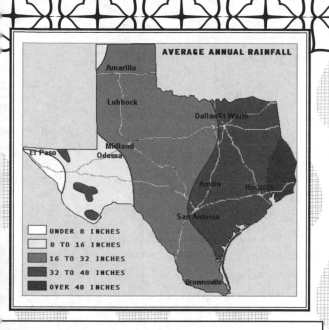

AVERAGE ANNUAL RAINFALL

UNDER 8 INCHES
8 TO 16 INCHES
16 TO 32 INCHES
32 TO 48 INCHES
OVER 48 INCHES

TEXAS PRECIPITATION

North American Precipitation

Now study the map that shows the annual precipitation of North America.

1. How does Texas's climate compare with other areas of North America?

_____

_____

2. Is Texas's precipitation typical of the central region of the United States? Explain.

_____

_____

_____

Precipitation is the amount of rain, snow, sleet, or any other form of water that is deposited in an area. Study the map here, which shows Texas's average annual precipitation.

1. How much precipitation does most of Texas receive in a year, on average?

_____

2. Which parts of Texas receive the highest amount of precipitation?

_____

3. Which part receives the lowest?

_____

Average Annual Rainfall
More than 96 inches
64 to 96 inches
32 to 64 inches
16 to 32 inches
8 to 16 inches
Less than 8 inches

© GeoNova

RIVERS AND WATER

Rivers

1. As you have already learned, there are many rivers in Texas. Here are some of those rivers explained. Find them on the map, right. Color them blue.

Red River: Runs along the Texas/Oklahoma Border.

Rio Grande: Longest river in Texas! Runs along the Texas/Mexico border.

Nueces River: Runs west of San Antonio from Edwards Plateau to the Gulf of Mexico.

Colorado River: 862-miles long and runs through the capital of Texas, Austin.

Trinity River: 710-miles long; longest river that runs entirely in Texas, from North Texas (DFW area) all the way down to Liberty and then the Gulf of Mexico.

Brazos River: Second longest river in Texas; runs from New Mexico through Texas and into the Gulf of Mexico.

2. Texas river systems also have very important tributaries. Tributaries are rivers that join and "contribute" to the flow of a major river. Four Texas tributaries are listed below. Find these rivers on the map and color them red.

Llano River

Pedernales River

Pease River

Clear Fork

3. Find the Llano Estacado on the map. Color it green.

4. The beginnings of rivers are called the headwaters. If all water flows downhill, then where are the headwaters of Texas's rivers located?

Some rainwater that doesn't evaporate seeps underground, into pores between sand, clay, and rock formations called aquifers. Aquifers are like underground water tanks that can be tapped into for daily consumption. Water moves through aquifers much like a glass of water poured onto a pile of sand. This "groundwater" provides about 60% of the water used by Texans. Natural springs are places where underground water comes to the surface. Barton Springs in Austin is a natural swimming pool whose waters stay at 68 degrees all year long!

Link to the Past

Our modern water system is based on the aqueducts of the Ancient Romans. Aqueducts resembled tall stone waterslides that relied on gravity to transport water from high in the hills down to the surrounding cities. Once the water reached the cities, it was stored in large cisterns that were just like our water towers. Then, the water would flow through pipes to houses and public fountains.

What about water towers? Water towers are a common site across Texas. Usually decorated with a particular city's logo, these structures are simple, but so important to everyday living. Each tower is designed to hold about a day's worth of water for the community it serves.

One tower might hold more than a million gallons of water. Towers are built on high ground to provide enough pressure to allow the water to flow up the pipes and into your home. What time of day do you think most of the water in a city's water tank is used? Why?

_____

_____

_____

_____

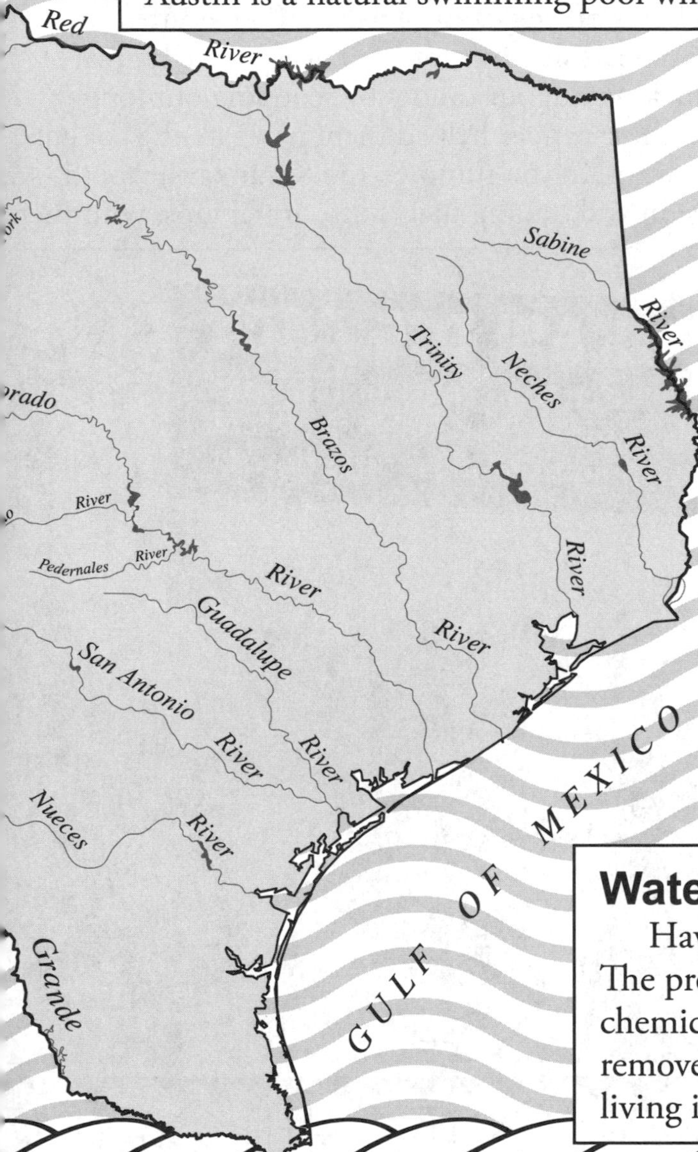

Map labels: Red River, Sabine River, Trinity, Neches, Brazos, River, Colorado, River, Pedernales River, River, Guadalupe, San Antonio River, River, Nueces River, Grande, GULF OF MEXICO

Water Takes a Bath

Have you ever wondered how the water you drink gets from nature to your faucet? The process is called water purification and involves several steps that clean up water. First, chemicals are added to remove bacteria and other sediments. Then, the water is filtered to remove any particles that remain. Next, the water is disinfected to kill any microorganisms living in the water. Finally, most communities add fluoride to water to prevent tooth decay!

NATIVE AMERICANS

Native American peoples not only provided Texas with its name, but also a rich cultural history. The very first Americans walked the land in search of food. Wooly mammoths and giant bison grazed the wide-open plains of North America. The meat from these animals fed many and their hides provided shelter and clothing.

Caddo

The Caddo lived in the pine forests of East Texas. They were the most advanced culture in the region and were very successful at farming, growing cotton, and making pottery. The Caddo would make a clearing in the forest to plant corn, beans, and squash. They built dome-shaped grass houses for many people to live in. Children were taught how to scrape seeds from sunflowers and pumpkins. Young people also learned how to weave strips of cane into mats and baskets.

Jumano

The Jumano people lived in West Texas in the Mountains and Basins region of the state. These Native Americans were known as farmers. Their land was dry, but the Jumano took water from nearby streams to water their crops. They lived in adobe villages called pueblos. They were also known to trade for goods that they could not grow or make themselves.

Karankawa

This Native American group lived along the coast of the Gulf of Mexico. They were known as nomads, which meant the Karankawa had no permanent home. Rather, they would move from place to place. During the cold winter months, the Karankawa would live on islands off the coast of Texas. They hunted fish and trapped shellfish for food. They were known for making dugout canoes by scooping out long logs. These canoes helped them navigate the coastal waterways. In the summer, the Karankawa would move inland, taking their huts, or wiklups, with them.

MY TEXAS! BIG FACT

Brewster is the largest county in Texas. It's roughly the same size as Connecticut, and Delaware could fit inside it three times!

MORE NATIVE AMERICANS

Comanche

The Comanche were strong warriors and hunters. Like the Karankawa, the Comanche were also a nomadic people who lived in tepees made from long poles covered with buffalo hides. An interesting note, it was the women who took down the tepees and put them back up. The buffalo was very important to the Comanche because they got everything they needed from it: food, clothing, and blankets. The Comanche were skilled at horseback riding too. In fact, the Comanche ruled the entire Central and Great Plains regions of Texas!

Apache

The Apache farmed for part of the year, and then after the crops came in, would move into a nomadic lifestyle and hunt and gather food. After horses were introduced to the Apache, they stopped being farmers and relied solely on hunting buffalo. The Apache were pushed south and southwest by the Comanche, resulting in two separate groups: the Mescalero Apache and the Lipan Apache.

Kiowa

The Kiowa lived primarily in the Texas panhandle and were nomads who also hunted buffalo. Like the Comanche, the women were in charge of moving the tepees. An entire village of tepees could be broken down and packed within an hour's time. A type of sled called a travois was used by the Kiowa people to transport supplies over land.

Indian Tools

Native American tribes from early Texas times used a variety of tools to get different jobs done. Like today, Indians had to hunt, gather, prepare, and cook food as well as build shelters for protection. Unlike our modern society, the Native American tools looked very different. Here are some of the tools they used:

- **Basket:** used to gather plants
- **Rock:** used as a hammer to grind things
- **Stone scraper:** used to trim wood or remove fat/flesh from animal hides
- **Flint:** used to cut flesh in meal preparation
- **Slivers of shell:** used as fishing hooks
- **Pointed stones:** used as arrowheads
- **Animal bone:** used as hoe blades when attached to wooden handles
- **Hollowed out tree stump (mortar) and long stick with large ends (pestle):** combined to grind corn into flour

MY TEXAS! BIG FACT

Texas measures 268,601 square miles and is only smaller than Alaska. This makes Texas bigger than every country in Europe!

NATIVE AMERICAN TOOL QUEST

Stone was a plentiful resource for Native Americans in Texas. They would carve and chip stones to make a variety of tools for all sorts of everyday jobs. For this activity, it will be your responsibility to (a) match the "tool" with its proper definition, and (b) draw what each tool should look like based on that definition.

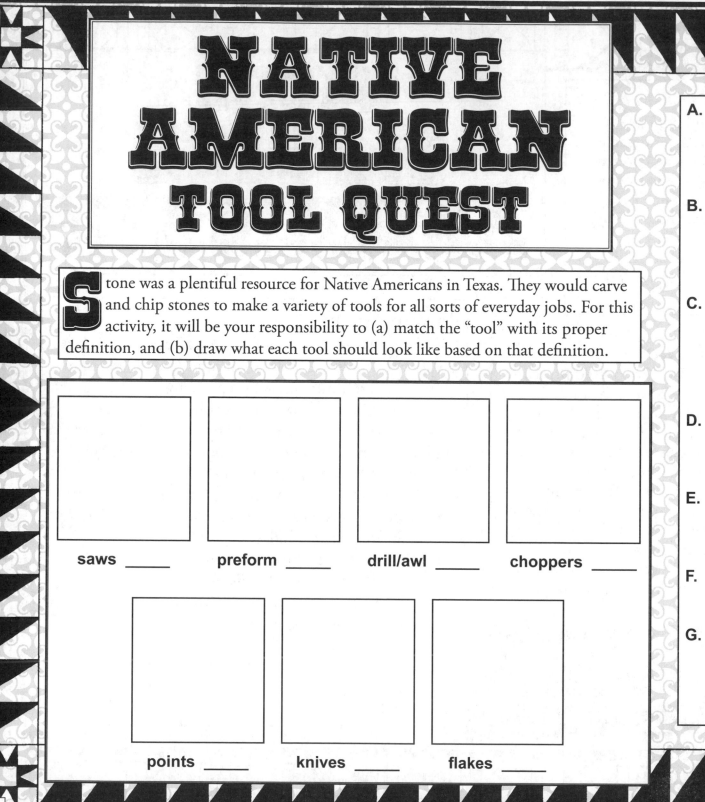

saws _____   preform _____   drill/awl _____   choppers _____

points _____   knives _____   flakes _____

A. This semi-carved stone was oval in shape with wavy edges. These lighter stones were easier to carry back to the village, where they would then be made into a specific tool.

B. This carved stone was blade-shaped, with a slight "hook" at one end. This tool would be used to dig up tubers, animals, and water. It could also be used to remove bark from trees.

C. Just like a tool found in our kitchen, this stone was carved to a sharp point on one end. The opposite end was wider to be used to hold the tool. This tool was used to cut and chop animal flesh and vegetables.

D. This tool was made just a bit larger than a penny with one sharp tip and the other end made to be tied onto an arrow or spear.

E. Roughly spherical in shape, one end of this tool was carved into a sharp edge while the other hand would be used as a handle.

F. This carved stone resembled big needles. This tool was used to make holes in things.

G. This tool was carved into a long, oval shape. Its edges had "teeth" carved into them so it could be used to cut wood and could also be used to scrape flesh off of animal skin.

SIX FLAGS

The first of the six flags belonged to the country of Spain. In 1519, Spanish explorer Hernando Cortés (also known as Hernán Cortés) landed in what is now Mexico. Nine years later, another explorer, Álvar Núñez Cabeza de Vaca (commonly called Cabeza de Vaca), landed in Tampa Bay (Florida). After landing, de Vaca and his fellow explorers got lost and couldn't find their ship. They built rafts and tried sailing along the coast hoping to reach Mexico. A storm blew the men off course and carried them to Galveston Island in Texas.

Spain

The second flag to fly over Texas belonged to France. In 1685, French explorer Robert de La Salle came to Texas. Several years before this, La Salle had claimed land around the mouth of the Mississippi River for France. He called this land Louisiana. He returned to France asking the king for permission to start a colony in Louisiana. When La Salle made his way back to Louisiana, his ship was blown 400 miles off course, causing him to land on the shore of Matagorda Bay on the Texas coast. He built a fort there and claimed the surrounding land for France.

France

Mexico

The third flag that flew over Texas belonged to Mexico. The land that makes up modern-day Texas was once Mexico. When the Spanish explorers landed in Mexico, the Spanish king began to rule over the Mexican people. In 1821, after a long war, Mexico gained its independence from Spain. In 1836, Mexican General Antonio López de Santa Anna made an effort to reclaim land that he believed still belonged to Mexico. Santa Anna defeated Texas troops at the famous battle of the Alamo in San Antonio, however he was later defeated and taken prisoner by Sam Houston's troops at the Battle of San Jacinto.

If you've heard the phrase "six flags over Texas," you probably know it's the name of a popular amusement park in Arlington, TX. This title comes from a very important part of Texas history. Each "flag" represented a country that claimed the land that is now Texas. Over the course of time, six different flags flew over Texas. In this section, you will learn some very interesting facts about how these flags were raised. Early explorers came to Texas in search of gold, in hopes of fulfilling the dream of amassing great wealth.

MORE FLAGS

Republic of Texas

The fourth flag to fly over Texas is the same flag that is the state's flag today—Repulic of Texas. From 1836–1845, Texas was an independent country. It had its own president, mail delivery, and army, among other things. The red, white, and blue flag with its single "lone" star flew over the republic as a symbol of freedom and individualism.

United States

United States. As you can see, Texas was its own republic for only 9 years. Financial burden took its toll, as well as ongoing clashes with Mexico that brought about the republic's downfall. Texas joined the Union as the 28th state in 1845.

Confederate States of America

Confederate States of America. Sixteen years passed after Texas joined the Union and trouble erupted in our country. The Civil War broke out between the northern and southern states. Texas decided to secede from the Union and join the South in the newly formed Confederate States of America. This new flag was called the "Stars and Bars" and was raised over Texas from 1861–1865. After the end of the Civil War, the United States flag was again raised with Texas's readmission to the Union in 1865.

Explorer Routes. You've learned what flags flew over Texas. Now add that information to the map below to trace the path each explorer took in bringing his country's flag to Texas. Choose a color for each of the explorers listed in the legend, then use the Internet if you need help recreating the route each took to arrive in Texas.

Legend
Cabeza De Vaca (1527–1528)
Francisco Vásquez De Coronado (1541)
Robert de La Salle (1684)
Alonso Álvarez de Pineda (1519)
Henri de Tonti (1689)
Juan de Oñate (1598)

DESIGN THE FLAGS

SPAIN

FRANCE

MEXICO

REPUBLIC OF TEXAS

UNITED STATES

CONFEDERATE STATES OF AMERICA

Now it's time to put it all together. In each of the six boxes, draw one of the flags that flew over Texas. The boxes have been labeled to help you get started, but use the Internet and other sources to help you find a good picture of each of the flags.

MY TEXAS! BIG FACT

Texas is the only state to have the flags of six different nations fly over it: Spain, France, Mexico, the Republic of Texas, the Confederate States of America, and the United States.

FRONTIER LIFE

It's hard to imagine living life on the Texas frontier as a young boy or girl. There was no Internet, smartphones, cars, or television. The floor of a pioneer house was covered in dirt, not carpet or wood. There was no electricity, let alone video games! No vacuums or dishwashers. No running water or bathrooms. Outside, threats came in the form of bears, panthers, coyotes, droughts, and floods. Indian raids and prairie fires were also harsh realities.

1. What would you like about being a frontier boy or girl?

_____

_____

2. What would be the scariest thing about living on the frontier?

_____

_____

3. What would be the hardest thing about living on the Texas frontier?

_____

_____

4. What kind of games would you create to have fun with your friends on the frontier?

_____

_____

Daily Schedule

Here's a brief look at a day in the life of a pioneer boy or girl. Think about how different your life is! On the blanks below, you can write what you do during that specific hour of the day. You should write down times that match your schedule.

Time of Day	Boy	Girl	Me
Sunrise	fetch water	milk the cows	
	bring in wood	boil water	
	rake ashes from fireplace	help make breakfast	
	eat breakfast	eat breakfast	
	weed garden	clean house and wash clothes	
		make soap	
Midday	eat lunch	eat lunch	
	hunt (rabbit)	gather vegetables	
	gather hay, cow dung, and wood for fire	collect eggs	
Evening		milk cows	
		help make dinner	
	eat dinner	eat dinner	
	school (at home)	school (at home)	
	playtime	playtime	
	bedtime	bedtime	

Other jobs that you would be responsible for (depending on your age!) include grinding grain, sewing clothes, chopping and hauling wood, babysitting, churning cream to make butter, making candles, snapping peas, and protecting your pumpkins, potatoes, and squash from the hungry deer, gophers, and crows.

CATTLE DRIVES

From 1865 to 1886, there was a high demand for beef, so Texas ranchers needed a way to move their cattle to the north and the railroads. More than 20 million cattle were moved on these drives, proving how important this trade was to the economy. People who wanted to be part of a cattle drive could take on one of many positions, including trail boss (1), point man (2), swing (2), flank (2), drag (3), wrangler (1), and chuck wagon cook (1) who also helped with medical needs.

Label the diagram below with the correct names that match the correct post.

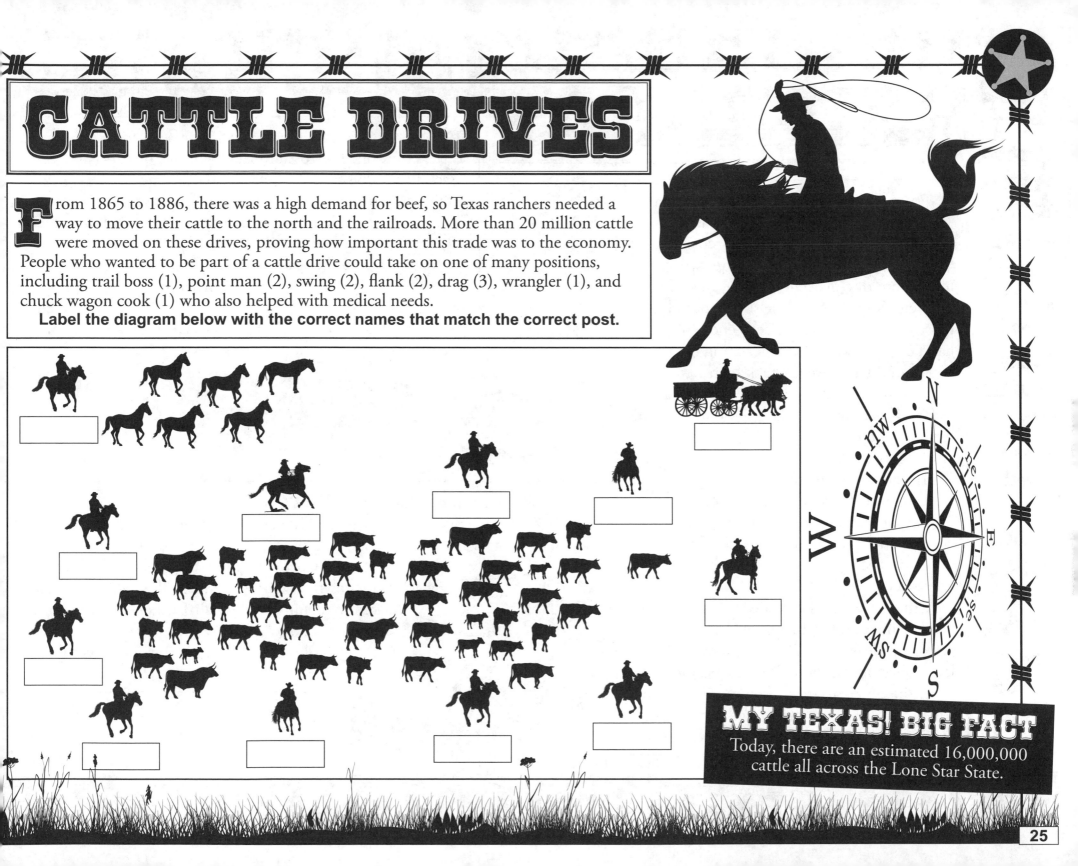

MY TEXAS! BIG FACT
Today, there are an estimated 16,000,000 cattle all across the Lone Star State.

RAILROADS

Even as late as 1850, most people who settled in Texas lived in the eastern portion of the state and all along the Gulf Coast. Transportation, or how people move from one place to another, was a huge problem. There were some steamboats, but most Texas rivers weren't deep enough to handle this mode of transportation on a year-round basis. Roads back then were not as smooth and well-maintained as they are today. If there were roads, they were made of dirt, meaning they couldn't be ridden over after a good hard rain.

The answer came to be a major part of the economic boom and development of Texas. Railroads would allow people and goods to travel long distances in a fraction of the time it previously took on wagon or horseback.

Cities grew and flourished along the railroad lines and in turn provided many job opportunities. Many of these "boomtowns" faded away just as quickly as they came, but others became thriving communities that are still here today. One such city that was born as a railroad stop is Bryan, TX.

The first track finished in 1853 ran a short 20 miles from Houston, TX, to Stafford, TX. Just 20 years later, Texas had 1,068 miles of railroad! By the end of 1891, nearly 9,000 miles of track had been laid and trains were operated by 42 rail companies. The peak of the railroad growth came in 1932 when Texas had 17,078 total miles of track!

In addition to the steam engines, Texas saw roughly 500 miles of track laid for electric interurban trains. These new trains help transport passengers between urban centers such as the Dallas-Fort Worth and Houston-Galveston connections.

MY TEXAS! BIG FACT
Texas leads the nation in railway mileage.

Two major developments of the 20th century brought about the decline of railroads in Texas. One of these was the car (and subsequent construction of interstate highways). By 1930, automobiles became affordable for many people, giving them more freedom to travel on their own. The other came in the 1960s with the advent of commercial jet airplanes. These airplanes allowed cargo as well as people to be transported over long distances at much quicker speeds than the railroads.

BLACK GOLD

Instructions: Look at the diagram of a Texas oil derrick. Your job is to correctly label the different parts: derrick, drill string, drill bit, drill collar, casing. Use the Internet if you get stuck!

Oil is a big part of Texas history. Like the Gold Rush of 1849, the oil boom brought people from all over the world to Texas in search of fame and fortune. "Black gold" was found in wonderful abundance by Pattillo Higgins in Spindletop, TX, in 1901. About 100,000 barrels of oil a day flowed 150 feet high into the Texas sky uncapped for 9 days. An economic and social frenzy came to Beaumont soon after this enormous discovery.

It has been documented that one man had tried selling some land in the area for $150 for 3 years. After the oil flowed, he sold the property for $20,000. The buyer turned around, and within 15 minutes, resold the same property for $50,000! Beaumont's population soared from 10,000 people to 50,000. By 1902, the oil wells produced 17,500,000 barrels of black gold.

Oil storage facilities, pipelines, and refineries popped up in Beaumont, Port Arthur, and Sabine Pass. Modern petroleum companies like Texaco and Exxon were started at Spindletop.

How about oil and everyday life? Can you think of commonly used products that come from oil? Have you seen women wearing make-up? Cosmetics are made up of about 80% petroleum-based products. Whether you walk to school, ride the bus, or drive in a car, oil goes with you. The synthetic rubber found in sneakers and tires are made from oil. The asphalt that the bus or car drives on is a solid form of petroleum. The soaps used in your dishwashers and washing machines are made with glycerin, which is made from petroleum. Plastic soda bottles, video game consoles, and water bottles are all made from oil. Ink, dice, footballs, hand lotion, shampoo, paint, trash bags, crayons, guitar strings, balloons, and vitamin capsules are just a handful of everyday things that are made from oil! And, last but not least, gasoline!

ANIMALS OF TEXAS

The **armadillo** is the small state animal of Texas. Its name in Spanish means "little armored one." These creatures love to dig for food like ants, grubs, and termites, and they build burrows to live in. If an armadillo gets surprised, it will jump 3–4 feet in the air!

The **longhorn** is the large state animal of Texas. These iconic cattle have horns that can grow up to 7 feet long. These animals were imported to Texas by Spanish settlers. Longhorns are beef cattle whose meat is lean and lower in fat than other cows.

Bats also live in Texas. In fact, 32 types of bat have been discovered in Texas, the most in the United States! There is a place in Texas called Bracken Cave where there are believed to be 20 to 40 million bats. Bats feed on mosquitoes and bugs that eat crops. Bats also live in urban areas too! In Austin, TX, there is a place called the Congress Avenue Bridge that is home to the largest urban bat colony in the United States. There are between 750,000 and 1.5 million bats during the peak of the spring and summer seasons.

Black bears also live in Texas. These are one of the largest mammals in North America. Adult black bears stand as tall as a 6-foot man.

Bobcats are found all over Texas, while mountain lions are now limited to the mountainous regions of the western part of the state. Exotic jaguars once roamed the land, but are most likely extinct.

The **coyote** resembles a small wolf and preys on livestock. It helps farmers by eating rodents and rabbits that threaten crops. Coyotes are found all over Texas. They are fast and smart. They "talk" to each other by barking in high, shrill barks. These animals tend to hunt in pairs and have taken to night hunting.

White-tailed deer and mule deer live also live in Texas. These gentle creatures eat green plants and other vegetation. People gave the mule deer its name because of its huge floppy ears that resemble the ears on the mules that pioneers used to pull their wagons west.

Texas is known for its **bass** that live in rivers and lakes. Largemouth bass are usually green with a band of horizontal dark splotches along the middle of their bodies. The spotted bass are popular in East Texas in rivers such as the Sabine, Neches, and Cypress. The Guadalupe bass is only found in Texas and is also the state fish.

1. How many of pictures. Here black bear, blu rabbit, longho squirrel, weasel

2. If you live in T

Many mor in Texas. example, weasels, badgers, raccoons. In the crappie, bluegill,

Choose one a not described on and find out mor Summarize what lines below.

_____
_____
_____
_____
_____
_____
_____
_____

imals pictured here can you name? Write the names beside the
e animals included: alligator, armadillo, badger, bald eagle, bat,
obcat, catfish, copperhead, coyote, Guadalupe bass, hawk, jack
llard duck, mule deer, prairie dog, porcupine, raccoon, skunk,
e-tailed deer, wolf.

ut a star beside all the animals that live in your area of the state.

als live
nd, for
olves,
s, and
ive catfish,
her fish.
that is
pages,
t it.
rn on the

Johanna July

One animal not on our list that is very important to Texas is the mustang. Commonly referred to as wild horses, mustangs are free-roaming horses that were first brought to this country by Spanish colonists. By the early 1900s, there were roughly two million mustangs roaming the plains of North America.

Soon, Native Americans would capture these horses and use them as their primary means of transportation, but in order for the mustangs to be used they had to be broken.

One famous Texan known for her horse-breaking skills was Johanna July. Johanna and her family were part of the Seminole tribe, and she had a lot of experience taming horses. Johanna had a very unique way of getting the job done. Her home was near the Rio Grande, and she would lead a horse into its wide waters. Johanna would then swim up, grab the horse's mane, and gently ease on to the horse's back. The horse, exhausted from swimming, soon lost the strength to buck.

Reptiles and Amphibians

The first reptiles to roam Texas were the dinosaurs, including the Paluxysaurus (official state fossil) and the Alamosaurus. Today, Texas's reptiles are much smaller than their prehistoric counterparts. The most common are lizards, snakes, toads, and frogs. One kind of snake that helps farmers is the bull snake. It is not poisonous and loves to eat mice and other rodents that eat crops stored for winter.

Garter snakes live in gardens and shady places where they can find and eat insects. Gardeners like garter snakes because they eat the bugs that like to chew up the plants in backyard gardens. These snakes are not poisonous and are usually so small that they can hide among the leafy vegetables.

The most well-known snake in Texas is probably the copperhead. These snakes have gray and brown bands and copper-colored heads. Copperheads are known as venomous snakes because their fangs contain a poison called venom that can make a person very ill or even die. This venom helps the snake stabilize its prey and make it easy to catch.

Another popular reptile in Texas is the horned lizard. These interesting creatures have an alias, "horned frogs." This is the mascot for Texas Christian University in Fort Worth. When attacked, the horned lizard will puff its body up, which causes its body scales to protrude. This makes it hard to swallow. Another bizarre defense mechanism for the Texas horned lizard is the ability to squirt a stream of blood out of the corners of its eyes. Obviously, this confuses the attacker, giving the lizard a second chance at life.

INSECTS OF TEXAS

1. How many insects pictured on these pages can you name? Write the names beside the pictures. Here are the insects included: ant, beetle, bumblebee, cockroach, cicada, cricket, dragonfly, earwig, firefly, grasshopper, ladybug, locust, mantis, Monarch butterfly, moth, spider, tick, yellow jacket.

2. If you live in Texas, put a star beside all of the insects that live in your area of the state.

There are more than 25,000 different kinds of insects that make their home in Texas. Insects have segmented bodies, three pairs of legs, and one pair of antennae. When they are adults, most insects have wings. Insects can be as majestic as butterflies, as plain as grasshoppers, as irritating as mosquitoes, or as musical as crickets. They provide food for birds, reptiles, and some mammals.

Butterflies

The official insect of Texas is the Monarch butterfly. It has beautiful orange wings with black borders and white speckled dots along its edges. The Monarch migrates through Texas on its way to Mexico.

Color the wings of the Monarch butterfly in the picture.

MY TEXAS! BIG FACT
More species of bats live in Texas than in any other part of the United States.

The Scorpion

There are more than 15 scorpion species in Texas. The average size of these venomous insects is around 2 inches. The most common one found in Texas is the striped bark scorpion, which can be found in crevices under rocks, in old barns and sheds, and hiding out in vegetation. They are known for their curved erect tails that contain their stingers. This particular species will glow under ultraviolet light, giving it a supernatural appearance. Although not lethal, this scorpion's sting is very painful.

Mosquitoes

Texans love outdoor activities like cookouts, camping, and hiking. During the summer months (and sometimes beyond depending on the weather!), these fun times can be overshadowed by the presence of mosquitoes. Most mosquito bites just itch, but some can be harmful. There is a sickness called West Nile virus transmitted by mosquitoes that can cause death.

Many people have devised ways of dealing with these pesky insects. For example, mosquitoes that carry disease tend to be active between dusk and dawn. Therefore, people often limit their amount of outdoor activity during these hours. Some people install ornamental ponds and stock them with fish that eat mosquitoes! Research another way people avoid mosquito bites and describe one of these methods below. (You might ask an adult to describe his or her favorite method. Or, share a mosquito defense your family or neighbors use.)

_____

_____

_____

_____

Web Mania!

In science class, you have learned that a food web is a graphic that shows the path energy takes through a food chain. Your job is to place the correct animal or insect in the correct bubble to complete the food web. Here are the names to place: **snake**, **rabbit**, **mouse**, **owl**, **coyote**, **frog**, **bird**, **beetle**, **butterfly**, and **grasshopper**. Draw arrows to show what eats what. Remember, your arrows should show the energy flow through the web (this means your arrows will point from the prey to the predator). Ask a parent for help if you get stuck!

BIRDS AND PLANTS

Wildflowers

Since 1901, the bluebonnet has been the state flower of Texas, beating out the cactus for the title. Bluebonnets have been dotting the wide-open spaces of the state for a long time. Native Americans used the bluebonnet as a part of their folklore, while the Spanish priests grew the flower around their missions. In 1930, the Texas Highway Department implemented a beautification program and planted bluebonnets all along the state's many roadways. Today, Texans from all over the state seek out the roadside bluebonnet fields to take family pictures.

A fun fact associated with the bluebonnet is that people say it's illegal to pick them. This has grown into an urban legend, but is simply not true. It's just proof how important the bluebonnet is to Texas culture!

A host of other colorful wildflowers dot the Texas countryside, including milkweed, columbine, oxeye daisy, firewheel, orange coneflower, and Indian paintbrush.

Plants

Elm, crape myrtle, oak, pecan, pinyon, sycamore, walnut, jacaranda, and Douglas fir are just a few of the many trees found in Texas. The pecan tree was named the state tree in 1919. It can grow to 100 feet tall and can survive more than 1,000 years. Native Americans relied on the pecan as an everyday food staple. Today, eating pecan pie is a Texas tradition!

MY TEXAS! BIG FACT

The city of Tyler, TX, hosts the world's largest rose garden. The 22-acre garden contains 38,000 rose bushes representing 500 varieties of roses.

Birds

The Texas state bird is the mockingbird. This light gray flyer is only about 10 inches long, but is a fierce protector of its nest and territory. The name mockingbird comes from the bird's ability to "mock" or copy the songs of other birds.

The peregrine falcon is an amazing predator. It can reach speeds of 200 miles an hour as it dives for its prey. Another "bird of prey" found in Texas is the red-tailed hawk. This hawk has a cry that sounds like a scream, which it uses when hunting or when another hawk comes into its territory.

Some birds in Texas are threatened or endangered. That means that if they are not protected, they may disappear from the Earth. The bald eagle, whooping crane, brown pelican, and Northern Aplomado Falcon are all endangered birds of Texas.

NAME GAME

Directions. Just for the fun of it, find the name of a Texas city or town to fit each definition below. These definitions are tricky! Ask your family to help you out. Hints: Some of the answers are based on how a town is pronounced, not how it is spelled. Some items have more than one correct answer.

1. Name of a chess piece: _____
2. Animal that once roamed the prairies: _____
3. Capital of Greece: _____
4. Part of a flower: _____
5. Kind of pear: _____
6. Where Fenway is located: _____
7. Capital of Georgia: _____
8. Desert plant: _____
9. Sailed the ocean in 1492: _____
10. Home of the NFL Browns: _____
11. Brand of sneaker: _____
12. Expensive dishes: _____
13. There's a grand one in Arizona: _____
14. Another word for heavenly: _____
15. Author of A Christmas Carol: _____
16. Opposite of late: _____
17. One of the sisters in Frozen: _____
18. Garden where Adam and Eve lived: _____
19. Third planet from the sun: _____
20. Name of a carnival wheel: _____
21. Icy Jack's last name: _____

22. Sparkly strand wrapped over a Christmas tree: _____
23. Orange trees grow in this: _____
24. Popular NASCAR driver (#24): _____
25. River in New York: _____
26. Not haughty or full of pride: _____
27. European country that resembles a boot: _____
28. Third president of the United States: _____
29. Miss Piggy's green friend: _____
30. Pioneer dwelling crafted from trees: _____
31. Opposite of grumpy: _____
32. A small store: _____
33. Town where Jesus grew up: _____
34. To think about: _____
35. Office supply store with an EASY button: _____
36. Main dish at Thanksgiving: _____
37. Not sure: _____
38. Quick eye movement: _____
39. Cardinal direction (left on a map): _____
40. Now you make up a definition! _____

_____

_____

IMMIGRANTS

Native Americans. Native Americans were the very first people to live on the land that became known as Texas. It was the Karankawas who the Europeans first came into contact with.

Caddo, Tonkawa, Natchitoches, Hasinai, Jumano, Coahuiltecan, Apache, and Comanche were other Native American tribes that inhabited this land. Today, this culture is still alive and well in Texas. Three federally recognized tribes are located in the Lone Star State: the Alabama-Coushatta tribe (in Livingston, TX); the Kickapoo Traditional Tribe (in Eagle Pass, TX); and the Ysleta del Sur Pueblo (in El Paso, TX).

Germans. Germans first arrived in Texas around 1831, but in 1842, thousands of Germans arrived in Galveston. They mostly settled in Central Texas. Today, they represent the third-largest national-origin group in the state.

Italians. Between 1880 and 1920, a flood of Italian immigrants came to Texas in hopes of providing their families a good standard of living. Farming and mining were the primary jobs for this group, while others worked building railroads and opened up small businesses in urban areas.

Mexicans. Over the centuries, people came to Texas to find better living and agricultural opportunities. As far back as 1710, Mexico claimed the frontier land that is now Texas. Only the Rio Grande separates Texas and Mexico, so the people and culture have blended together. Today, a popular food choice for Texans is called "Tex-Mex." This cuisine is characterized by shredded cheese, beef, beans, spices, and tortillas. Fajitas, grilled and spiced meats often eaten with tortillas, is a great tasting Tex-Mex creation found in restaurants all across the state. Chalupas and enchiladas are also delectable dishes that Texans enjoy.

French. Early French immigrants were traders with Native Americans, while many more arrived in Texas after the Louisiana Purchase. These settlers came from France to seek better social, political, and economic conditions.

African Americans. Many African Americans first arrived in Texas against their will as slaves.

The first Anglo Americans in Texas moved from the South where the unfortunate practice of slavery was commonplace. By 1850, 48,000 African Americans were enslaved in Texas. On April 9, 1865, the Civil War ended, which also meant the end of slavery in the United States. However, it wasn't until 2 months later, on June 19, 1865, that word finally reached Texas that all slaves were to be freed. This important day became known as "Juneteenth" and is still celebrated in Texas with festivals and other celebrations.

English. In 1821, Stephen F. Austin started a colony in Texas. Families from England who had originally settled in other parts of the country came to Texas as a part of Austin's new colony. These colonists were given land to grow crops—families who agreed to be farmers received 177 acres of land, while families who would be ranchers received 4,428 acres!

Czech. The first Czech immigrants did not come to Texas until 1852. These people were farmers who first arrived in Galveston and soon settled across the Coastal Plains. The Czechs took pride in their farming skills and went on to play an important part of the cotton industry. Today, this culture is on full display in the town of West, TX. Opened in 1983, the "Czech Stop," located off Interstate 35, treats travelers to mouth-watering kolaches, strudels, and sweet breads.

Spanish. From 1716 to 1821, the Spanish occupied Texas. Many important crops were introduced by them, including wheat, oats, barley, onions, peas, and watermelons. Animals, including cattle, horses, and hogs were also brought here by the Spanish. Farming and irrigation techniques were improved upon by Spanish missionaries and settlers. Spanish is a second language for millions of Texans; for some it is the first language. For example, many items in Texas grocery stores are labeled with nutrition facts and cooking instructions in both English and Spanish.

Homesteaders. In 1862, President Lincoln signed the Homestead Act, which allowed people to claim 160 acres of land out west. To get the land, families had to agree to "prove up" (improve) the land by planting and harvesting a crop as well as building a house, barn, and corrals. People from all over came to homestead land in the Midwest.

From 1836 to 1876, Texas had its own version of this plan, which gave out more than 4 million acres of land to encourage people to live here.

MY TEXAS! BIG FACT

Waco, TX, was where the first Dr Pepper soda was sold in 1885. The number of cans sold each year in Texas alone could wrap around the Equator more than 8 times!

Each one of us is connected to the past through our ancestors. Some of us know a lot about our ancestors, and some of us do not. Write about one of the subjects below. (You may want to ask your parents, grandparents, or other relatives for help.)

1. **How you came to be in Texas (or the state you live in).** When, how, and why did you and/or your family come to Texas (or the state you live in)? Was it recently? Was it a long time ago? Where did your family come from? Which part of Texas (or the state you live in) did your family settle in? Explain.

2. **Your ancestors.** Write about your ancestors. Did they immigrate to the United States? Were they Native Americans? What did they do to earn a living? Where did they live? What else do you know about them? What makes you proud of them?

3. **A story about a certain ancestor.** Tell a story about one of your ancestors. Has a story about one of them been handed down from generation to generation in your family? Can your grandparents tell you a story about their parents? Is there a story connected to a family recipe, a quilt, or a piece of furniture, for example? Write about what you discover.

_____

_____

_____

_____

_____

_____

_____

_____

FAMOUS TEXANS

Many fascinating people have lived in Texas. Look over the list below and choose someone who sounds interesting to you. (You may also choose someone not on the list. There are many famous Texans!) Find out more about the person you have selected, using the library, your local museum, the Internet, interviews with people who have known the person, or other sources. Create a profile of the person on page 37.

Babe Zaharias: Famous female golfer

Barbara Jordan: First African American elected to the Texas Senate and later a U.S. Representative

Bob Denver: Star of "Gilligan's Island" show

Charles Goodnight: The best-known rancher in Texas

Chester W. Nimitz: A Fleet Admiral of the U.S. Navy

Cleto Rodríguez: Won Medal of Honor, Silver Star, Bronze Star, and Purple Heart awards for his military bravery

Dan Rather: American journalist and news anchor

David Crockett: Took part in the Battle of the Alamo

Doris Miller: Known for his courage during the attack on Pearl Harbor

Dwight D. Eisenhower: 34th president of the United States

Edna Gladney: Early proponent of children's rights and adoption services

Elisabet Ney: Famous sculptor and art pioneer

Gail Borden, Jr.: Inventor of condensed milk

Gene Roddenberry: Creator of the original "Star Trek" TV series

George Bush: 41st President of the United States

George W. Bush: 43rd President of the United States

Ginger Rogers: Danced with Fred Astaire in 10 musical films

Greenbury Logan: Freed Black soldier in the Texas Revolution

Henry Cisneros: Former mayor of San Antonio and U.S. Secretary of Housing and Urban Development

Ila Loetscher: Known as the Turtle Lady and was also a pilot who flew with Amelia Earhart

Isamu Taniguchi: Created a beautiful Japanese garden in the city of Austin

Jane Long: Known as "The Mother of Texas"

Jesse Chisholm: Built a number of trading posts along the cattle drive trail that bears his name

Johanna July: Tamed wild horses by riding them into the Rio Grande

John T. Biggers: Muralist who founded the art department at Texas Southern University

José Navarro: Friend of Stephen Austin, and a fellow founding father of Texas

Joseph Glidden: Farmer who patented the barbed wire

Juan Seguín: Commanded troops in the Texas Army's battle for independence

Katherine Stinson: Fourth woman in the United States to obtain a pilot's certificate

Lady Bird Johnson: Former First Lady of the United States

Lyndon Johnson: 36th President of the United States

Mary Kay Ash: Founder of Mary Kay Cosmetics

Mirabeau B. Lamar: Second President of the Republic of Texas

Ninnie Baird: Fort Worth baker who went on to found Mrs. Baird's Bakeries

Nolan Ryan: Holds the Major League Baseball record with 5,714 strikeouts

Pattillo Higgins: Geologist who led the oil drilling expedition at Spindletop

Quanah Parker: Last of the Comanche chiefs who was influential to many people

Richard King: Riverboat captain and founder of the King Ranch in South Texas

Roger Staubach: Dallas Cowboys quarterback who led them to two Super Bowl wins

Roy Bedichek: A Texas writer, naturalist, and educator

Sally Ride: First American woman in space

Sam Houston: First and third President of the Republic of Texas

Scott Joplin: African-American composer famous for his ragtime compositions

Selena Perez: Singer-songwriter known as "the Queen of Tejano music"

Stephen F. Austin: Known as the Father of Texas for successfully colonizing the region

Susanna Dickinson: Along with her baby, was one of the two American survivors of the Alamo attack

Tommy Lee Jones: Popular actor who has won an Academy Award

Walter Cronkite: Was a popular news anchorman for the CBS Evening News

William "Bill" Pickett: Cowboy and rodeo performer

PROFILE OF

_____

Name

_____

Years of birth and death

What did the person you have chosen accomplish in his or her life? What is the person noted for? Explain.

_____

_____

_____

_____

_____

_____

_____

_____

_____

What is the most interesting thing you found out about this person? Explain.

_____

_____

_____

_____

_____

In the space above, draw a picture of the person you have chosen. Or make a copy of a photograph to paste in the space.

Directions: How many answers can you find to the puzzle, right? For each category listed along the side of the puzzle, see if you can think of an appropriate word that begins with the letter at the top of the column. Give yourself one point for each item you list.

Yes, you can list more than one item in a box, and it's okay if you can't find an answer for some boxes. Feel free to get help from reference books, the Internet, your family, or other sources. To help you get started, some items have been filled in for you.

	M	Y	T	E	X	A	S
Places in Texas		Yorktown					
Things related to sports and recreation		Yoga					
Things in a toy box		Yo-yo					
Animals and birds you might find in Texas		Yellow-Bellied Sapsucker					
Unit of measurement		Yard					
You pick the category!							

TEXAS PARKS, MONUMENTS, AND HISTORICAL SITES

Texas has two national parks, a national seashore, and several historical sites and monuments. Find out about them by using tourist brochures, the Internet, reference books, maps, and people you know.

Match the descriptions on the left with the parks and monuments on the right. Write the number of each description on the lines below the correct park or monument's name. There will be more than one answer for each park. Items #1 and #2 have been completed for you, as examples.

1. Longest stretch of undeveloped barrier island in the world
2. Named after cowboy "Allie Bates"
3. Its main attraction has been used for scrapers, knives, and tools
4. Pinery Station of the Pony Express is here
5. Contains the highest point in Texas
6. Located in the Texas Panhandle
7. Includes the spectacular canyons of Santa Elena, Mariscal, and Boquillas
8. Marine pollution is studied here
9. Located near El Paso
10. Geologist Wallace Pratt contributed almost 6,000 of its acres
11. Arrowheads can be made here
12. Contains the Chihuahuan Desert
13. Corpus Christi is a popular city here
14. Showcases a massive limestone formation known as "El Capitan"
15. Also known as "La Isla Blanca"
16. Merges desert and mountain ecosystems
17. Known for its extensive hiking trails
18. Visitors tour its quarries
19. Ranching is a big use of this land
20. Gets its name for a "turn" in the Rio Grande River
21. Lies in Brewster County
22. Contains more than 80 species of butterflies
23. The U.S. Navy once had a bombing range here
24. Located on the Texas boundary with Mexico

Guadalupe Mountains National Park

_____

Big Bend National Park

_____

Padre Island National Seashore

_____

Alibates Flint Quarries National Monument

_____

Choose one of the following parks or monuments listed below. Using books, pamphlets, or other sources, find out more about the park or monument. Then summarize one fact or interesting piece of information. Lyndon B. Johnson Historical Park; Fort Davis; Chamizal National Memorial; Big Thicket National Preserve; Palo Alto Battlefield; San Antonio Missions

_____

_____

_____

TEXAS A TO Z

Directions. Remember those alphabet books you used to read when you were little? Imagine you are making an alphabet book just for Texas. Think of at least one Texas item for each letter of the alphabet. For example, you might consider names of people, places, events, animals, or plants. Write your alphabet items beside the letters below. Here are some examples to get you started:

Amarillo
Beaumont
Corpus Christi

A _____

B _____

C _____

D _____

E _____

F _____

G _____

H _____

I _____

J _____

K _____

L _____

M _____

N _____

O _____

P _____

Q _____

R _____

S _____

T _____

U _____

V _____

W _____

X _____

Y _____

Z _____

MY TEXAS! BIG FACT

The deadliest natural disaster in U.S. history was the Galveston hurricane of 1900, which killed between 6,000–12,000 people.

RURAL AND URBAN TEXAS

People who live in cities or towns live in urban areas. People who live in the country live in rural areas. People who grow crops, raise livestock, and produce food are also called rural. How would you define yourself—rural or urban? Why?

_____

_____

_____

_____

_____

_____

Population density. Population density refers to the average number of people per square mile living in an area. When there are many people per square mile, an area is considered urban. When there are few people per square mile, an area is considered rural.

The population densities of six Texas counties are listed below. Suppose that a population density of 100 or more people per square mile indicates that a county is urban. Label each of the counties as "urban" or "rural," based on its population density:

_____ **Harris County:** 2,460 people per square mile

_____ **Lubbock County:** 269 people per square mile

_____ **Presidio County:** 1.9 people per square mile

_____ **Bexar County:** 1,408 people per square mile

_____ **Sherman County:** 4 people per square mile

_____ **Zapata County:** 13 people per square mile

Rural Texas. More than 75% of the land in Texas is made up of farms and ranches. The people who live on the farms and ranches are involved in agriculture. Agriculture refers to producing crops and raising livestock.

Texas farmers and ranchers produce crops and raise livestock that are used throughout the state, the nation, and the world. Sometimes we don't think about the connection between a product we buy in the store and where it came from. Look at the following list of some of the animals raised in Texas. Draw a line matching each animal with the items that we buy from a store, listed on the right.

| cattle |

| sheep |

| hogs |

| chicken |

bacon

blankets

yogurt

chicken nuggets

leather shoes

eggs

footballs

hand lotion

ham

wool sweaters

See if you can think of eight more items in your home that are produced from the animals listed.

1. _____

2. _____

3. _____

4. _____

5. _____

6. _____

7. _____

8. _____

Texas farmers raise many crops. Some of the most commons ones are listed below, along with the counties that produce most (not all!) of these crops. Follow the instructions after each item, using the county map, right.

- **Counties where onions are grown:** Frio, Dimmit, La Salle, Webb, Zavala, Val Verde, Williamson, Kerr. Shade these counties purple.

- **Counties where watermelons are grown:** Brewster, Williamson, Brooks, Cameron, Duval, Hidalgo, Starr, Zapata. Shade these counties red.

- **Counties where blueberries are grown:** Crockett, Sabine, Williamson, Concho, Milam, DeWitt. Shade these counties blue.

- **Counties where potatoes are grown:** Parker, Real, Sterling, Williamson, Brazos, Montgomery, Galveston. Shade these counties brown.

- **Counties where corn is grown:** Dallam, Hartley, Sherman, Castro, Moore, Falls, Williamson, Hansford, Parmer, Bell. Shade these counties green.

- **Counties where apples, cantaloupe, peaches, and grapefruit are grown:** Aransas, Montgomery, Victoria, Refugio, Matagorda, and Brazoria. Shade these counties light green.

- **Counties where pumpkins grow:** Navarro, Tarrant, Hood, Wise, Parker. Shade these counties orange.

1. **Count up the counties.** Which county produces more crops than the others? _____

2. **Look at the counties that border the Gulf of Mexico.** What observation can you make about farming in this part of the state? _____

   _____

3. **Think about your observation from Question 2.** Why do you think these particular crops grow in these counties more than in other parts of the state? _____

   _____

4. **If you live in Texas, find the county where you live.** Circle it. Are there crops grown in your county? If so, write them on the line provided. _____

MY TEX
BIG FA

Texas is divided
254 counties. T
most in the Uni

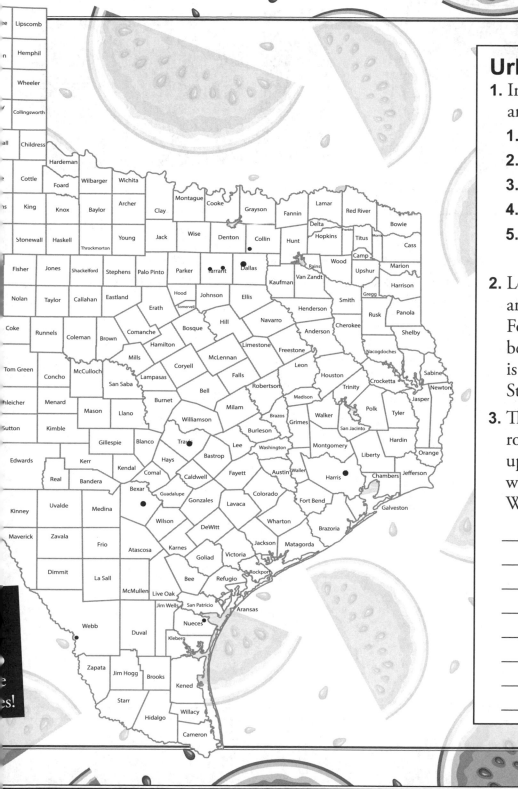

Urban Texas

1. In order from largest to smallest, the largest urban areas in Texas are:

1. Houston
2. San Antonio
3. Dallas
4. Austin
5. Fort Worth
6. El Paso
7. Arlington
8. Corpus Christi
9. Plano
10. Laredo

2. Locate the cities mentioned above on the Texas map on the left and draw a rectangle around the cities of Dallas, Arlington, and Fort Worth. The area that you boxed is called the Metroplex because it is the economic and cultural hub of North Texas. It is also the largest land-locked metropolitan area in the United States.

3. The way people move from one place to another plays a very big role in the location of cities and towns. Many Texas cities grew up where a trail crossed a river, where two trails met, or the place where two rivers met. Choose two Texas cities. Study a map. Why do you think they might have grown up where they are?

_____

_____

_____

_____

_____

_____

_____

SPORTS AND RECREATION

Professional Sports

Professional sports are very popular in Texas. You have probably seen Texas teams play on television. You may have even seen them play in person. Who are the professional teams in Texas? Write the name of each team in the correct space below. Then either draw or paste in a picture of each team's logo.

Football (NFL): _____

Football (NFL): _____

Basketball (NBA): _____

Basketball (NBA): _____

Basketball (NBA): _____

Basketball (WNBA): _____

Basketball (WNBA): _____

Baseball (MLB): _____

Baseball (MLB): _____

Hockey (NHL): _____

Soccer (MLS): _____

Soccer (MLS): _____

- **How many of these teams have you seen play in person?** _____

- **Who is your favorite professional player on a Texas team?** _____

Texas is a gigantic state with many fun, recreational opportunities within its borders. Many people come to Texas to visit the state and enjoy all it has to offer. In fact, the tourist industry is very important to the economy of Texas.

Look at the list below. All of these activities are possible in Texas! Put a star beside each activity you have tried. Circle up to three that you would like to try some day. What items can you add to this list?

Birding	Hot air ballooning
Camping	Kiteboarding
Canoeing	Long distance running
Fishing	Mountain biking
Golfing	Skydiving
Hiking	Swimming
Horseback riding	Tubing

MY TEXAS! BIG FACT
The state animal of Texas is the armadillo. They always have four babies—either four boys or four girls. That's a lot of armadillos!

Texas High School Football
Texas is known for many things, but when it comes to sports, high school football is king. Current NFL players who played high school football in Texas include Andy Dalton, Josh McCown, Andrew Luck, Dez Bryant, Von Miller, Matthew Stafford, Robert Griffin III, and Drew Brees. That's a great deal of talent! There was even a book written about Texas high school football called Friday Night Lights. Many school districts spend a lot of money building football stadiums for their students and families to enjoy.

Waterpark Heaven
Texas is also known for its hot summers. To combat this, Texas has many waterparks to let visitors cool off and have a blast when temperatures get high. One such park, Schlitterbahn (voted best waterpark in the country), is a Texas favorite with parks in New Braunfels, Galveston, South Padre, and Corpus Christi.

In Arlington, TX, Hurricane Harbor is another massive waterpark waiting to give visitors slippery thrills with a reported 3 million gallons of water! And the fun doesn't stop there. Texas also is home to Hawaiian Falls, which has seven parks around the state to offer refreshing pools during heat waves!

ROAD TRIP

Imagine that you are going to take a road trip around Texas to learn more about its interesting places, exciting history, and beautiful landscapes. Plan your trip, following the directions below.

1. **Decide on 10 places in the state that you wish to visit.** Use the list at the right for suggestions. (You may also choose other places that are not listed.) Be sure to include the following in your 10 places:
   - At least one place in the Mountains and Basins region
   - At least one place in the Great Plains region
   - At least one place in the Central Plains region
   - At least one place in the Coastal Plains region
   - At least one place in a big city
   - At least one place in a rural area

2. **Find your 10 places on a road map of Texas.** If you were driving, which highways and roads would you take?

3. **List your itinerary on page 48.** An itinerary is an outline of a trip. It lists the places you will go, in the order that you will visit them.

4. **Draw a few postcards from the places you "visited."** Use the boxes provided on page 48.

Bonus challenge. Use a road map to determine approximately how many miles you will drive on your trip and how many hours you will spend traveling. Write your distance and time in the box on page 48.

Just a Few Places to Visit in Texas

State and national parks/monuments: Alibates Flint Quarries National Monument, Big Bend National Park, Guadalupe Mountains National Park, Padre Island National Seashore, San Jacinto Battlegrounds and Monument, Dinosaur Valley State Park, Enchanted Rock State Natural Area, Seminole Canyon, Lake Brownwood, Sea Rim State Park, Mission Tejas, Possum Kingdom, Caprock Canyons State Park and Trailway, and Old Tunnel State Park.

Other attractions:
- **Amarillo:** Big Texan Steak Ranch, Cadillac Ranch, Frontier Texas!, The Grace Museum.
- **Austin:** LBJ Library, Bob Bullock Texas State History Museum, State Capitol, Barton Springs Pool, Mount Bonnell, Lady Bird Johnson Wildflower Center.
- **Canyon:** Panhandle-Plains Historical Museum.
- **Corpus Christi:** USS Lexington, Texas State Aquarium.
- **Dallas:** Dallas Arboretum and Botanical Gardens, Meyerson Symphony Center, Sixth Floor Museum/ Texas School Book Depository, Perot Museum of Nature and Science.
- **Del Rio:** Whitehead Memorial Museum.
- **Edinburg:** Museum of South Texas History.
- **El Paso:** National Border Patrol Museum, Railroad and Transportation Museum.
- **Fort Davis:** McDonald Observatory.

Places to Visit, continued

- **Fort Worth:** Bass Performance Hall, Fort Worth Zoo, Fort Worth Stockyards, Fort Worth Museum of Science and History.
- **Galveston:** Bishop's Palace, Moody Gardens, Lone Star Flight Museum, The Strand Shopping District.
- **Goliad:** Goliad State Park and Historic Site.
- **Grapevine:** Great Wolf Lodge.
- **Harlingen:** Iwo Jima Memorial Museum.
- **Houston:** Children's Museum of Houston, Johnson (NASA) Space Center, Houston Zoo, Galleria Mall.
- **Huntsville:** Texas Prison Museum.
- **Kemah:** Kemah Boardwalk.
- **Kingsville:** Depot Railroad Museum.
- **Lubbock:** American Wind Power Center.
- **Marfa:** Marfa Lights Viewing Station.
- **New Braunfels:** Natural Bridge Caverns, Schlitterbahn.
- **San Antonio:** Alamo Mission, Riverwalk, Six Flags Fiesta Texas, Sea World, Witte Museum.
- **Waco:** Dr Pepper Museum, Cameron Park, Texas Ranger Hall of Fame, Mayborn Museum Complex.
- **Washington:** Star of the Republic Museum.
- **Victoria:** The Texas Zoo.

MY TEXAS! BIG FACT

Texas was an independent nation from 1836 to 1845. When it was annexed in 1945, it retained the right to fly its flag at the same height as the national flag.

TRIP ITINERARY

There are many wonderful places to go in Texas.
Use the space below to list your destinations.

1. _____
2. _____
3. _____
4. _____
5. _____
6. _____
7. _____
8. _____
9. _____
10. _____

BONUS CHALLENGE

1. How many miles you will drive on your trip?

Total Trip Mileage: _____

2. If you travel an average of 60 miles per hour, how many hours will you spend traveling?

Total Hours of Traveling Time: _____

DESIGN YOUR POSTCARDS

TEXAS HISTORY IN THE

Although you may not stop to think about it, history is being made every single day of the year. Events and people making headlines today will appear in history books 40 or 50 years from now.

MY TEXAS

Corn dogs are believed to hav
Germany wanted to jazz up
is a part of Texas tradition. A
sells more than 600,000 corn
a line of corn dogs that coul

AS
ORY
AKING

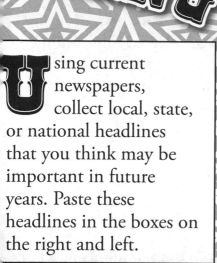

Using current newspapers, collect local, state, or national headlines that you think may be important in future years. Paste these headlines in the boxes on the right and left.

G FACT

ed when early Texans from sages. Today, the corn dog fair, Fletcher's Corn Dogs 24 days. That would make from Dallas to Galveston!

TEXAS GOVERNMENT

National Government

Texas sends two senators to serve in the United States Senate in Washington, DC.

Who are the two current senators?

1. _____

2. _____

Texas sends 32 representatives to serve in the United States House of Representatives.

Which representative serves the people in the congressional district where you live?

_____

County Government

Texas is so big it is divided into 254 counties!

If you live in Texas, which county do you live in? If you live in a different state, pick a place in Texas you'd like to visit and find the name of the county. Then use that county when answering the other questions in this section.

_____

There are five people who govern each county called a Commissioners' Court.

One member is always the county judge and the other four are elected commissioners. If you live in Texas, find out the names of the people on your county's Commissioners' Court. If you live outside of Texas, pick a county to research the names.

County Judge: _____

Elected Commissioners:

1. _____   3. _____

2. _____   4. _____

The town where the Commissioners' Court meets is called the county seat.

It is also where the courthouse is located. What is the name of the county seat of your county? _____

State Government

Governors of Texas are elected to serve for 4 years.

Who is the current governor of Texas?

_____

The Texas Legislature is made up of the House of Representatives and the Senate.

How many members make up:

- The House? _____

- The Senate? _____

Why do you think there are more members in the House than there are in the Senate?

_____

_____

_____

_____

Town and City Government

Many Texans are also citizens of a town or a city and elect local officials.

If you live in a Texas town or a city, who is the mayor?

_____

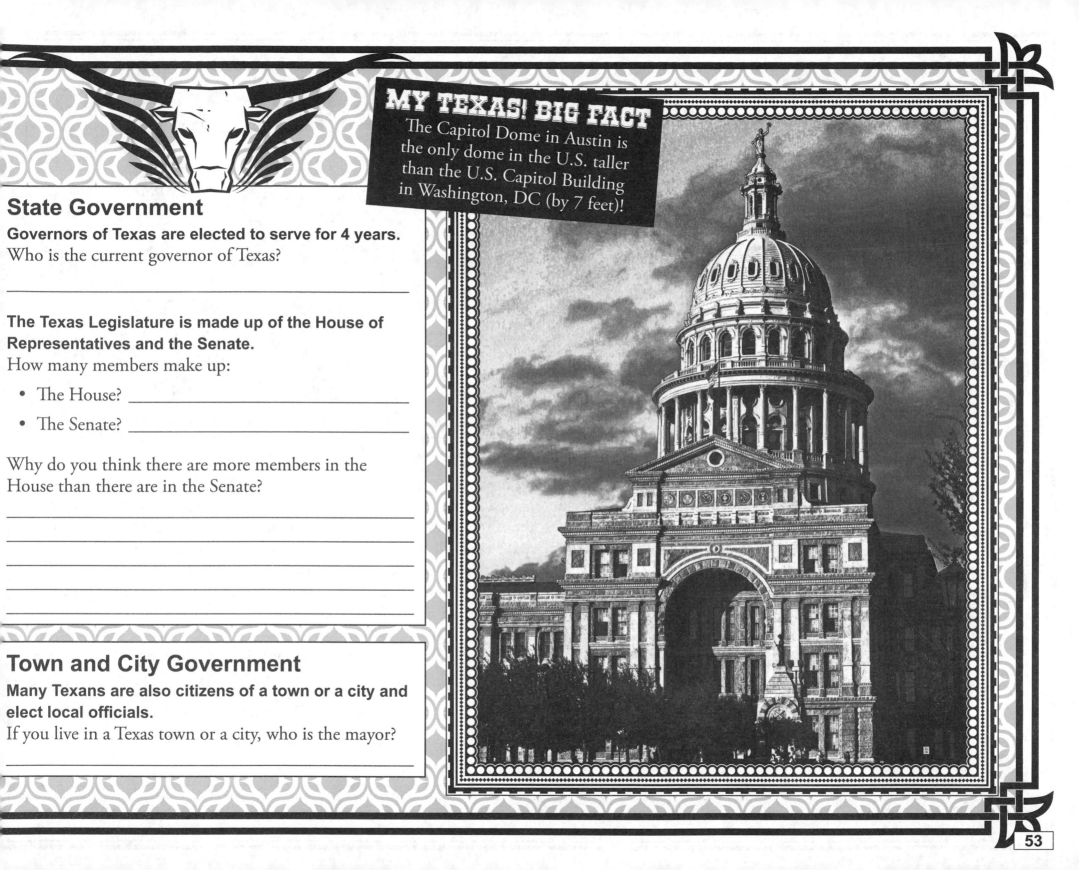

TEXAS UNIVERSITIES

You've learned a lot about the great state of Texas. As you get older, you will learn about American history and even world history. Along the way, you will see how Texas is just a piece of a much bigger puzzle. Even though it might seem like a long way away, after high school you will have an opportunity to go to college. This is where you get to major in a particular subject and learn about the skills for a job that you might like to do for a living.

People go to college to become doctors, lawyers, teachers, nurses, engineers, geologists, and so much more. Texas has many outstanding colleges all across the state. You might be familiar with some of them because a family member has gone there or maybe you've seen a certain college's sports teams on television.

Match them up! Below is a scrambled list of locations and mascots of some of the major universities in Texas. Match the location and mascot to the university. Then, using the map to the right, match the correct college with the corresponding marker on the map. To help you get started, some items have been filled in for you. Put a star by any of the schools that a family member has attended. Circle the markers for the universities you might be interested in attending. Remember, you're not too young to start thinking about where you'd like to go to college!

Waco	Wildcats	Lubbock	Mustangs	Austin
College Station	San Marcos	Eagles	Red Raiders	Houston
Dallas	Aggies	Bearkats	Abilene	Bears
Fort Worth	Bobcats	Longhorns	Huntsville	Cougars
Denton	Horned Frogs			

Use the lines below to write down any questions you might have about college. Take them to your parents or teacher and have them help you answer them.

_____

_____

_____

_____

_____

_____

_____

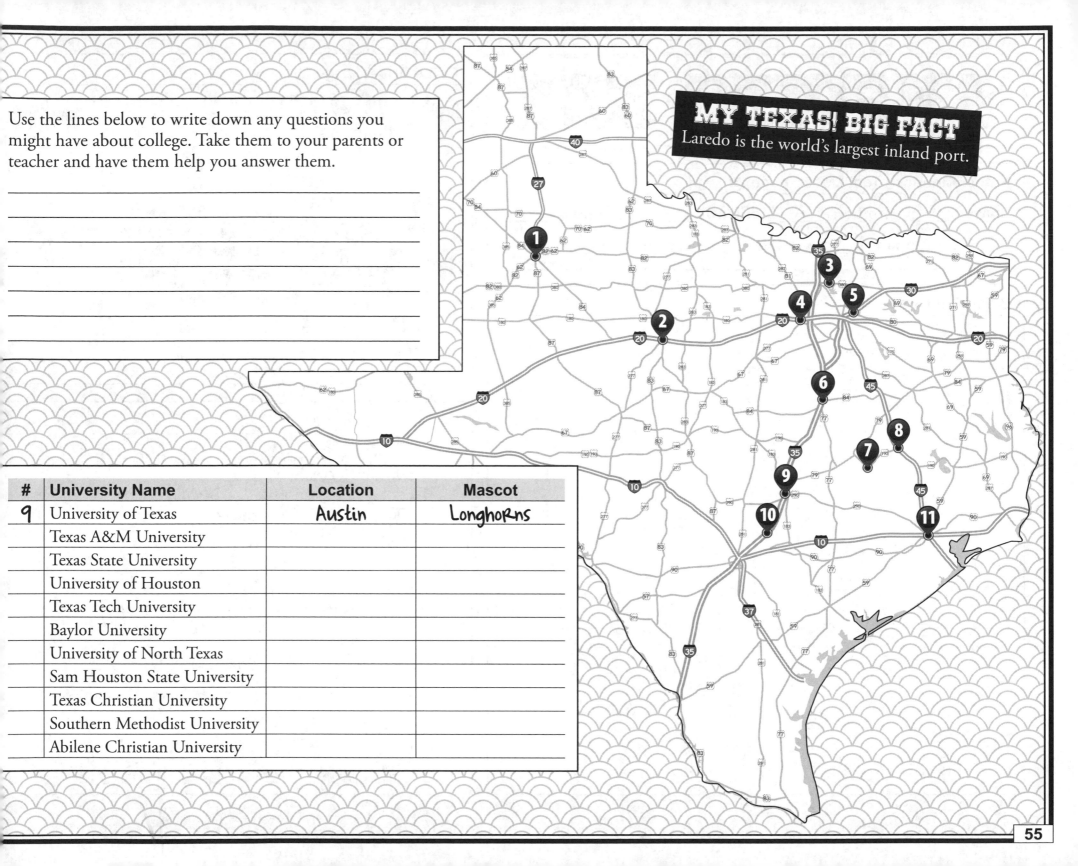

#	University Name	Location	Mascot
9	University of Texas	Austin	Longhorns
	Texas A&M University		
	Texas State University		
	University of Houston		
	Texas Tech University		
	Baylor University		
	University of North Texas		
	Sam Houston State University		
	Texas Christian University		
	Southern Methodist University		
	Abilene Christian University		

ANSWER KEY

Native American Tool Quest, page 20

saws __G__   preform __A__   drill/awl __F__   choppers __E__

points __D__   knives __C__   flakes __B__

Black Gold, page 27

derrick

casing

drill string

drill collar

drill bit

Cattle Drives, page 25

Wrangler

Chuck Wagon

Swing

Point

Flank

Drag

Trail Boss

Drag

Drag

Flank

Point

Swing

Web Mania!, page 31

owl

coyote

snake

bird

mouse

frog

beetle

Rabbit

butterfly

grasshopper